Please return this book on or before the date shown above. To renew go to www.essex.gov.uk/libraries, ring 0345 603 7628 or go to any Essex library.

Essex County Council

What is SOUND?

First published in 2018 by Wayland
Copyright © Hodder and Stoughton 2018

Wayland
Carmelite House
50 Victoria Embankment
London EC4Y 0DZ

Managing editor: Victoria Brooker
Creative design: Paul Cherrill

ISBN: 978 1 5263 0668 5

Printed in China

MIX
Paper from
responsible sources
FSC® C104740
FSC
www.fsc.org

Wayland is a division of
Hachette Children's Books,
an Hachette UK company.
www.hachette.co.uk

What is

SOUND?

Written by
KAY BARNHAM

Illustrated by
MIKE GORDON

WAYLAND

'Hurry up!' Dad shouted from the doorstep.
'We're late for school again.'
Iris and Ava clattered noisily down the stairs.

'Sorry!' they said, hurrying outside.
Dad slammed the front door behind them. BANG!
'Come on,' he said. 'We're going to have to run!'

They raced along the pavement past the roadworks. Thud-thud. Thud-thud. Thud-thud went the digger.

Drrrrrrr, drrrrrrr went the drill.

'Quick!' shouted Dad, as an ambulance wailed past. Nee-naw.
'What?' cried Iris. 'Everything is too LOUD. I can't hear you!'

'Quick!' yelled Ava. 'And you're supposed to say "pardon", not "what"!'

9

At school, Iris's teacher taught the class
about sound. 'It's a type of energy,' said Mrs Gibbs.
'Sound happens when an object vibrates, like this
drum.' She banged the drum and the children
watched its flat surface wobble.

'The vibrations make sound waves,'
the teacher went on. 'When the sound
waves reach our ears, we hear sound.'

Iris was puzzled. 'But I didn't see any waves,' she said.

'Sound waves are usually impossible to see,' replied Mrs Gibbs. 'But if we could see them, they would look like this.' She began to draw on the board.

'With deep sounds, the waves
travel slowly. They are far apart.'

'High sounds make faster sound waves.
These are much closer together.'

'Let's go on a sound trek!' said Mrs Gibbs, leading the children out of the classroom.

The saucepans clanged in the school kitchen.

In their PE lesson, children shouted, 'Oof!'

The headteacher sneezed. Aa-aa-atchoo!

Iris heard so many loud sounds, she ran
out of space to write them down.
'Loud sounds make big sound waves,'
said Mrs Gibbs.

In the school library, the sounds were quiet
ones. There was the soft noise of pages
being turned. Books were slid off shelves
with swishes and swooshes.

Children murmured quietly to each other,
until the librarian frowned.
'Soft sounds make small sound waves,'
whispered Mrs Gibbs.

17

On the way home from school, car horns honked, engines revved and dogs barked. Ava sang a song she'd learned at school. There were so many different sounds.

'How do we hear sounds?' Iris asked Dad.
'That's what your ears are for,' he replied.
'But you'll have to ask Mum how ears work.
She's the expert.'

Mum was a doctor. She told Iris that
the ear has three main parts.
'The outer ear is the part of the ear we can
see,' said Mum. 'It collects sound waves.
These travel into the middle ear, where
they make the eardrum vibrate.'

'Like the drum at school!' said Iris.
Mum nodded. 'And when the eardrum vibrates,
it makes the tiny bones next to it vibrate too.
These are called the hammer, the anvil
and the stirrup.'

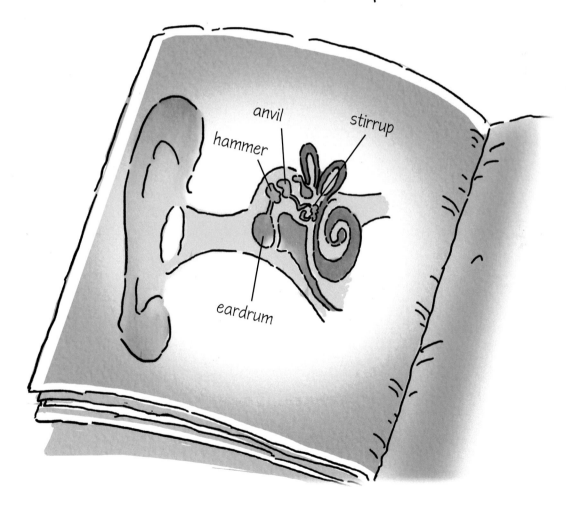

anvil

stirrup

hammer

eardrum

'What's the third part of the ear?'
asked Iris. 'What happens there?'
'Aha!' said Mum. 'That's the inner ear. Here, you'll
find the cochlea – a tube curled like a snail's shell.

'It's filled with liquid and lined with tiny hairs.
Vibrations from the middle ear make the liquid
move – and the tiny hairs too. The hairs send
messages to the brain, which turns them
into the sound that you hear!'
'Wow,' said Iris, completely amazed.

At the weekend, Mum took Iris
and Ava to the park.
'Watch how fast I can run!' shouted Ava.
She sprinted around the pond and across
the grass. 'Yoohoo!'

'Mum,' said Iris thoughtfully. 'When Ava was right beside me, her voice was loud. But now she's far away, her voice much quieter. Why?'

'Watch,' said Mum. She picked up a stone and threw it into the pond. Plop! 'See how the water ripples move outwards? That's how sound waves work. At first, the sound waves are big. Yet the further they travel, the smaller and smaller the waves become.'

'So if you are far away from
a loud noise, it sounds quiet?'
asked Iris. 'Exactly,' said Mum.

That afternoon, Dad got his record decks out.
'Come on, you guys,' he said. 'Get your dancing
shoes on. I need to practise for a gig!'
Everyone cheered.

'It's great having a DJ for a dad!' said Iris.
Soon, they were all dancing to super cool tunes.
'These are the sounds I like best,' said Dad.
'Musical ones!'

NOTES FOR PARENTS AND TEACHERS

The aim of this book is to introduce children to scientific concepts in an entertaining, informative way. Here are some ideas for activities that will encourage them to think further about sound — and have fun doing it!

ACTIVITIES

1. Make a list of all the different sounds in this book.
Now put them in order, from quietest to loudest.

2. Go on your own sound trek.
How many different sounds can you collect?

3 Can you rearrange these anagrams
to find five words to do with sound?

SUNDAE VOW

TRIVIA SNOB

RARE MUD

OR DUEL

ONE IS

SOUNDWAVE, VIBRATIONS, EARDRUM, LOUDER, NOISE

SOUND EXPERIMENT

You only hear sound waves when they enter your ear.
So when people work in very noisy places, they use ear defenders
to stop the sound getting into their ears and harming them.

Ask someone to stand at the other side of a room and SHOUT LOUDLY.
Then cover your ears with different materials to see which makes
things quieter.

You could try: Foam • Books • Cushions • Wood • Cardboard

Which material is best at blocking sound? Why do you think this is?

DID YOU KNOW ...?

Sound is measured in
decibels. It is named after
Alexander Graham Bell,
who invented the telephone.

A cochlear implant is
an electronic device that
helps deaf people to hear.

Fireworks can be as
loud as 150 decibels,
but a blue whale is
louder. The sounds
it makes measure
up to 188 decibels!

BOOKS TO SHARE

Sound
(*Boom Science* series)
by Georgia Amson-Bradshaw
(Wayland, 2018)

Sound
(*Science in a Flash* series)
by Georgia Amson-Bradshaw
(Watts Publishing, 2018)

Sound
(*Fact Cat* series)
by Izzi Howell
(Wayland, 2018)

Sound
(*Moving Up with Science* series)
by Peter Riley
(Watts Publishing, 2016)